THIS
JOURNAL
HOLDS THE HEARTFELT
PRAYERS AND THOUGHTS OF

FAITH · TRUTH · LOVE · BELIEVE · BLESS · PRAY · PEACE · JOY · HOPE · REJOICE · GRACE · HONOR

Welcome to the Wonderful World of Prayer Journaling!

Prayer is communication with our Creator. It encourages us to tap into the holiest parts of ourselves as we seek to develop an ever-deepening relationship with God. It's an opportunity for us to share our innermost thoughts and feelings and listen for God's guidance. Prayer is a way of connecting with God and acknowledging that we are part of something larger than ourselves. It may not result in a particular outcome, but it is always an opportunity for communion with our Creator.

There are four major types of prayers: gratitude (thank you), praise (awe), confession (I'm sorry), and supplication (please...), any of which you can include on the pages of this journal. Prayer journaling allows us to connect with God in a creative way. A regular prayer journaling practice can help us become more aware of our blessings as well as the ways the Holy One works in our life.

My Prayer Journal is divided into three sections:

- My Prayer List is a place to record people you are praying for, and why they are in your prayers.

- Prayer pages include places to write what you are grateful for and what you are praying for, supplemented by guided prayer pages to help you focus your prayers and occasional reminders to prompt you to check your Prayer List and Prayer Calendar.

- My Prayer Calendar is a perpetual coloring calendar on which you can record life-cycle events and other dates of importance to you and those you love.

Throughout the book you'll find art and hand-lettered scripture, along with sample prayers to inspire you. Many of the pages have room for you to add your own creative touches; you can color, doodle and decorate the designs as a hands-on prayer meditation.

Prayer journaling has made a big difference to me, and my hope is that this prayer journal will help you grow in your faith. May every step of your life's journey bring you closer to God, and may the prayers of your heart be answered and fulfilled.

Blessings always,

Joanne

My Prayer List

Make a list of specific people to pray for. Write down their names, and why you are praying for them. Pick a day of the week to review and update your list— and to pray for the people who are on it.

Date	Name	Reason

Date	Name	Reason

Date	Name	Reason

Date	Name	Reason

Date	Name	Reason

Date	Name	Reason

CELEBRATE
LIFE, GROWTH
& POSSIBILITY

Color a leaf for every wish you pray for a loved one.

MY *Prayers* FOR: _____

TODAY I AM ESPECIALLY GRATEFUL FOR:

_____
_____
_____
_____
_____

TODAY I AM PRAYING FOR:

_____
_____
_____
_____
_____
_____
_____
_____
_____
_____
_____

MY *Prayers* FOR: _____

TODAY I AM ESPECIALLY GRATEFUL FOR:

_____
_____
_____
_____
_____

TODAY I AM PRAYING FOR:

_____
_____
_____
_____
_____
_____
_____
_____
_____
_____
_____
_____

DATE

TODAY I PRAY:

TODAY I REGRET:

TODAY I AM IN AWE OF:

TODAY I AM GRATEFUL FOR:

MY *Prayers* FOR: _____
DATE

TODAY I AM ESPECIALLY GRATEFUL FOR:

_____

_____

_____

_____

_____

TODAY I AM PRAYING FOR:

_____

_____

_____

_____

_____

_____

_____

_____

_____

_____

_____

DATE _____

OPEN
YOUR
Heart TO
POSSIBILITY

TAKE
delight
IN THE
LORD
AND
HE SHALL
GIVE YOU
ALL THE DESIRES
OF YOUR
HEART

PSALM 37:4

Reminder:
CHECK YOUR PRAYER LIST!

MY  FOR: _____

DATE

TODAY I AM ESPECIALLY GRATEFUL FOR:

_____
_____
_____
_____
_____

TODAY I AM PRAYING FOR:

_____
_____
_____
_____
_____
_____
_____
_____
_____
_____
_____
_____

TODAY I PRAY:

TODAY I AM IN AWE OF:

TODAY I REGRET:

USE WHICHEVER TYPE OF
PRAYER FEELS RIGHT TO YOU

TODAY I AM GRATEFUL FOR:

MY Prayers FOR: _____

DATE

TODAY I AM ESPECIALLY GRATEFUL FOR:

_____

_____

_____

_____

_____

TODAY I AM PRAYING FOR:

_____

_____

_____

_____

_____

_____

_____

_____

_____

_____

_____

_____

MY  FOR: _____

TODAY I AM ESPECIALLY GRATEFUL FOR:

_____

_____

_____

_____

_____

TODAY I AM PRAYING FOR:

_____

_____

_____

_____

_____

_____

_____

_____

_____

_____

_____

_____

DATE

TODAY I PRAY:

TODAY I REGRET:

TODAY I AM IN AWE OF:

TODAY I AM GRATEFUL FOR:

MY *Prayers* FOR: _____

TODAY I AM ESPECIALLY GRATEFUL FOR:

_____
_____
_____
_____
_____

TODAY I AM PRAYING FOR:

_____
_____
_____
_____
_____
_____
_____
_____
_____
_____
_____

_____
DATE

LIVE
BY
INSPIRING
OTHERS
TO FLY

IS THERE SOMEONE IN YOUR LIFE
ESPECIALLY IN NEED OF PRAYER?

_____
_____
_____
_____
_____
_____
_____
_____
_____
_____
_____
_____

live
WITH
INTENTION

MY *Prayers* FOR: _____

TODAY I AM ESPECIALLY GRATEFUL FOR:

_____
_____
_____
_____
_____

TODAY I AM PRAYING FOR:

_____
_____
_____
_____
_____
_____
_____
_____
_____
_____
_____

DATE

TODAY I PRAY:

TODAY I AM IN AWE OF:

TODAY I REGRET:

USE WHICHEVER TYPE OF
PRAYER FEELS RIGHT TO YOU

TODAY I AM GRATEFUL FOR:

MY  FOR: _____

TODAY I AM ESPECIALLY GRATEFUL FOR:

_____

_____

_____

_____

_____

TODAY I AM PRAYING FOR:

_____

_____

_____

_____

_____

_____

_____

_____

_____

_____

_____

_____

MY *Prayers* FOR: _____

DATE

TODAY I AM ESPECIALLY GRATEFUL FOR:

_____
_____
_____
_____
_____

TODAY I AM PRAYING FOR:

_____
_____
_____
_____
_____
_____
_____
_____
_____
_____

DATE

TODAY I PRAY:

TODAY I REGRET:

TODAY I AM IN AWE OF:

TODAY I AM GRATEFUL FOR:

MY Prayers FOR: _____

DATE

TODAY I AM ESPECIALLY GRATEFUL FOR:

_____
_____
_____
_____
_____

TODAY I AM PRAYING FOR:

_____
_____
_____
_____
_____
_____
_____
_____
_____
_____
_____

DATE

A SINGLE *loving* ACT CAN TRANSFORM THE WORLD

TODAY I WILL TAKE RESPONSIBILITY FOR

_____
_____
_____
_____
_____
_____
_____
_____
_____
_____
_____
_____

Reminder:
CHECK YOUR
PRAYER CALENDAR

MY  FOR: _____

TODAY I AM ESPECIALLY GRATEFUL FOR:

_____
_____
_____
_____
_____

TODAY I AM PRAYING FOR:

_____
_____
_____
_____
_____
_____
_____
_____
_____
_____
_____
_____

DATE

TODAY I PRAY:

TODAY I AM IN AWE OF:

TODAY I REGRET:

USE WHICHEVER TYPE OF
PRAYER FEELS RIGHT TO YOU

TODAY I AM GRATEFUL FOR:

34

MY *Prayers* FOR: _____

TODAY I AM ESPECIALLY GRATEFUL FOR:

_____

_____

_____

_____

_____

TODAY I AM PRAYING FOR:

_____

_____

_____

_____

_____

_____

_____

_____

_____

_____

_____

_____

MY  FOR: _____

DATE

TODAY I AM ESPECIALLY GRATEFUL FOR:

_____

_____

_____

_____

_____

TODAY I AM PRAYING FOR:

_____

_____

_____

_____

_____

_____

_____

_____

_____

_____

_____

TODAY I PRAY:

TODAY I REGRET:

TODAY I AM IN AWE OF:

TODAY I AM GRATEFUL FOR:

MY *Prayers* FOR:

TODAY I AM ESPECIALLY GRATEFUL FOR:

_____

_____

_____

_____

_____

TODAY I AM PRAYING FOR:

_____

_____

_____

_____

_____

_____

_____

_____

_____

_____

DATE

DEAR
G♡D

PLEASE
BLESS
THOSE I
LOVE
AND
THOSE
THEY
LOVE

EACH
DAY IS A
GIFT TO BE
SHARED
WITH THOSE
WE LOVE

Reminder:
CHECK YOUR PRAYER LIST

MY  FOR: _____

DATE

TODAY I AM ESPECIALLY GRATEFUL FOR:

_____

_____

_____

_____

_____

TODAY I AM PRAYING FOR:

_____

_____

_____

_____

_____

_____

_____

_____

_____

_____

_____

DATE

TODAY I PRAY:

TODAY I AM IN AWE OF:

TODAY I REGRET:

USE WHICHEVER TYPE OF
PRAYER FEELS RIGHT TO YOU

TODAY I AM GRATEFUL FOR:

42

MY *Prayers* FOR: _____

TODAY I AM ESPECIALLY GRATEFUL FOR:

_____

_____

_____

_____

_____

TODAY I AM PRAYING FOR:

_____

_____

_____

_____

_____

_____

_____

_____

_____

_____

_____

_____

MY  FOR: _____

TODAY I AM ESPECIALLY GRATEFUL FOR:

_____
_____
_____
_____
_____

TODAY I AM PRAYING FOR:

_____
_____
_____
_____
_____
_____
_____
_____
_____
_____
_____
_____
_____

TODAY I PRAY:

TODAY I REGRET:

TODAY I AM IN AWE OF:

TODAY I AM GRATEFUL FOR:

MY *Prayers* FOR: _____

TODAY I AM ESPECIALLY GRATEFUL FOR:

_____

_____

_____

_____

_____

TODAY I AM PRAYING FOR:

_____

_____

_____

_____

_____

_____

_____

_____

_____

_____

_____

_____

_____
DATE

YOUR INNER LIGHT REFLECTS THE TRUE BEAUTY OF YOUR SOUL

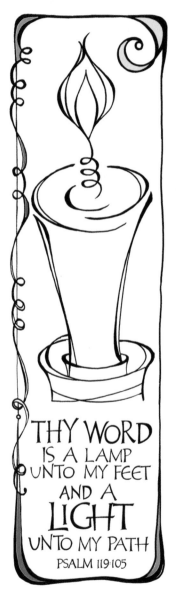
THY WORD IS A LAMP UNTO MY FEET AND A LIGHT UNTO MY PATH
PSALM 119:105

Reminder:
CHECK YOUR PRAYER CALENDAR

TODAY I WILL CARE FOR

_____
_____
_____
_____
_____
_____
_____
_____
_____
_____
_____
_____
_____
_____

MY  FOR: _____

DATE

TODAY I AM ESPECIALLY GRATEFUL FOR:

_____
_____
_____
_____
_____

TODAY I AM PRAYING FOR:

_____
_____
_____
_____
_____
_____
_____
_____
_____
_____
_____
_____

DATE

TODAY I PRAY:

TODAY I AM IN AWE OF:

TODAY I REGRET:

USE WHICHEVER TYPE OF
PRAYER FEELS RIGHT TO YOU

TODAY I AM GRATEFUL FOR:

MY  FOR: _____

TODAY I AM ESPECIALLY GRATEFUL FOR:

_____

_____

_____

_____

_____

TODAY I AM PRAYING FOR:

_____

_____

_____

_____

_____

_____

_____

_____

_____

_____

_____

_____

MY *Prayers* FOR: _____

TODAY I AM ESPECIALLY GRATEFUL FOR:

_____

_____

_____

_____

_____

TODAY I AM PRAYING FOR:

_____

_____

_____

_____

_____

_____

_____

_____

_____

_____

_____

_____

DATE

TODAY I PRAY:

TODAY I REGRET:

TODAY I AM IN AWE OF:

TODAY I AM GRATEFUL FOR:

MY  FOR: _____

TODAY I AM ESPECIALLY GRATEFUL FOR:

_____

_____

_____

_____

_____

TODAY I AM PRAYING FOR:

_____

_____

_____

_____

_____

_____

_____

_____

_____

_____

_____

_____

HAVE
FAITH
THAT
GOD'S
LIGHT
WILL
ILLUMINATE
YOUR PATH
NO MATTER
HOW DARK
THE NIGHT

Thank You

FOR BLESSING ME
WITH THE GIFT OF LIFE.

TODAY I WILL NURTURE SOMEONE BY

_____
_____
_____
_____
_____
_____
_____
_____
_____
_____
_____
_____
_____
_____

MY  FOR: _____

TODAY I AM ESPECIALLY GRATEFUL FOR:

_____
_____
_____
_____
_____

TODAY I AM PRAYING FOR:

_____
_____
_____
_____
_____
_____
_____
_____
_____
_____
_____
_____

DATE

TODAY I PRAY:

please

TODAY I AM IN AWE OF:

wow

TODAY I REGRET:

sorry

USE WHICHEVER TYPE OF
PRAYER FEELS RIGHT TO YOU

TODAY I AM GRATEFUL FOR:

Thanks

MY  FOR: _____

DATE

TODAY I AM ESPECIALLY GRATEFUL FOR:

_____

_____

_____

_____

_____

TODAY I AM PRAYING FOR:

_____

_____

_____

_____

_____

_____

_____

_____

_____

_____

_____

_____

_____

MY  FOR: _____

TODAY I AM ESPECIALLY GRATEFUL FOR:

_____
_____
_____
_____
_____

TODAY I AM PRAYING FOR:

_____
_____
_____
_____
_____
_____
_____
_____
_____
_____
_____

TODAY I PRAY:

TODAY I REGRET:

TODAY I AM IN AWE OF:

TODAY I AM GRATEFUL FOR:

MY  FOR: _____

DATE

TODAY I AM ESPECIALLY GRATEFUL FOR:

_____
_____
_____
_____
_____

TODAY I AM PRAYING FOR:

_____
_____
_____
_____
_____
_____
_____
_____
_____
_____
_____

DATE

THANK YOU GOD, FOR CREATING THE WORLD AND aLLOWING ME to LIVE IN it.

DRAW NEAR TO God & HE WILL DRAW NEAR TO YOU

Reminder:
IS THERE SOMEONE IN YOUR LIFE ESPECIALLY IN NEED OF PRAYER?

MY  FOR: _____

TODAY I AM ESPECIALLY GRATEFUL FOR:

_____
_____
_____
_____
_____

TODAY I AM PRAYING FOR:

_____
_____
_____
_____
_____
_____
_____
_____
_____
_____
_____
_____

TODAY I PRAY:

please

TODAY I AM IN AWE OF:

wow

TODAY I REGRET:

sorry

USE WHICHEVER TYPE OF
PRAYER FEELS RIGHT TO YOU

TODAY I AM GRATEFUL FOR:

thanks

MY *Prayers* FOR: _____
DATE

TODAY I AM ESPECIALLY GRATEFUL FOR:

_____
_____
_____
_____
_____

TODAY I AM PRAYING FOR:

_____
_____
_____
_____
_____
_____
_____
_____
_____
_____
_____
_____

MY  FOR: _____

TODAY I AM ESPECIALLY GRATEFUL FOR:

_____
_____
_____
_____
_____

TODAY I AM PRAYING FOR:

_____
_____
_____
_____
_____
_____
_____
_____
_____
_____
_____
_____

TODAY I PRAY:

TODAY I REGRET:

TODAY I AM IN AWE OF:

TODAY I AM GRATEFUL FOR:

MY *Prayers* FOR: _____

TODAY I AM ESPECIALLY GRATEFUL FOR:

_____

_____

_____

_____

_____

TODAY I AM PRAYING FOR:

_____

_____

_____

_____

_____

_____

_____

_____

_____

_____

_____

DATE _____

FIND A QUIET MOMENT EACH DAY TO RENEW YOUR SENSE OF WONDER

Life IS a SACRED JOURNEY

Reminder:
CHECK YOUR PRAYER LIST

MY  FOR: _____

TODAY I AM ESPECIALLY GRATEFUL FOR:

_____
_____
_____
_____
_____

TODAY I AM PRAYING FOR:

_____
_____
_____
_____
_____
_____
_____
_____
_____
_____
_____
_____

DATE

TODAY I PRAY:

please

TODAY I AM IN AWE OF:

wow

TODAY I REGRET:

sorry

USE WHICHEVER TYPE OF
PRAYER FEELS RIGHT TO YOU

TODAY I AM GRATEFUL FOR:

thanks

MY  FOR: _____

DATE

TODAY I AM ESPECIALLY GRATEFUL FOR:

_____

_____

_____

_____

_____

TODAY I AM PRAYING FOR:

_____

_____

_____

_____

_____

_____

_____

_____

_____

_____

_____

MY  FOR: _____

DATE

TODAY I AM ESPECIALLY GRATEFUL FOR:

_____

_____

_____

_____

_____

TODAY I AM PRAYING FOR:

_____

_____

_____

_____

_____

_____

_____

_____

_____

_____

_____

_____

DATE

TODAY I PRAY:

TODAY I REGRET:

TODAY I AM IN AWE OF:

TODAY I AM GRATEFUL FOR:

MY *Prayers* FOR: _____

TODAY I AM ESPECIALLY GRATEFUL FOR:

_____

_____

_____

_____

_____

TODAY I AM PRAYING FOR:

_____

_____

_____

_____

_____

_____

_____

_____

_____

_____

_____

_____

GOD
please
hear
my
PRAYER
even when
my heart is
at a loss
for words...

Believe

Reminder:
CHECK YOUR PRAYER LIST!

MY *Prayers* FOR: _____

TODAY I AM ESPECIALLY GRATEFUL FOR:

_____
_____
_____
_____
_____

TODAY I AM PRAYING FOR:

_____
_____
_____
_____
_____
_____
_____
_____
_____
_____
_____
_____
_____

DATE

TODAY I PRAY:

please

TODAY I AM IN AWE OF:

wow

TODAY I REGRET:

sorry

USE WHICHEVER TYPE OF
PRAYER FEELS RIGHT TO YOU

TODAY I AM GRATEFUL FOR:

Thanks

MY  FOR: _____

DATE

TODAY I AM ESPECIALLY GRATEFUL FOR:

_____
_____
_____
_____
_____

TODAY I AM PRAYING FOR:

_____
_____
_____
_____
_____
_____
_____
_____
_____
_____
_____
_____
_____

MY  FOR: _____
DATE

TODAY I AM ESPECIALLY GRATEFUL FOR:

_____
_____
_____
_____
_____

TODAY I AM PRAYING FOR:

_____
_____
_____
_____
_____
_____
_____
_____
_____
_____
_____

DATE

TODAY I PRAY:

TODAY I REGRET:

TODAY I AM IN AWE OF:

TODAY I AM GRATEFUL FOR:

MY *Prayers* FOR: _____
DATE

TODAY I AM ESPECIALLY GRATEFUL FOR:

_____
_____
_____
_____
_____

TODAY I AM PRAYING FOR:

_____
_____
_____
_____
_____
_____
_____
_____
_____
_____
_____
_____

LET
THE
BEAUTY
OF NATURE
inspire
YOUR
SOUL

THIS IS THE
DAY THE
LORD
HAS MADE

LET US
REJOICE
AND BE
GLAD
IN IT.

PSALM 118:24

TODAY I WILL NURTURE MYSELF BY

_____

_____

_____

_____

_____

_____

_____

_____

_____

_____

_____

_____

_____

Reminder:
CHECK YOUR
PRAYER CALENDAR

MY *Prayers* FOR: _____

TODAY I AM ESPECIALLY GRATEFUL FOR:

_____

_____

_____

_____

_____

TODAY I AM PRAYING FOR:

_____

_____

_____

_____

_____

_____

_____

_____

_____

_____

_____

_____

DATE

TODAY I PRAY:

TODAY I AM IN AWE OF:

TODAY I REGRET:

USE WHICHEVER TYPE OF
PRAYER FEELS RIGHT TO YOU

TODAY I AM GRATEFUL FOR:

MY *Prayers* FOR: _____

DATE

TODAY I AM ESPECIALLY GRATEFUL FOR:

_____

_____

_____

_____

_____

TODAY I AM PRAYING FOR:

_____

_____

_____

_____

_____

_____

_____

_____

_____

_____

_____

_____

MY  FOR: _____

DATE

TODAY I AM ESPECIALLY GRATEFUL FOR:

_____
_____
_____
_____
_____

TODAY I AM PRAYING FOR:

_____
_____
_____
_____
_____
_____
_____
_____
_____
_____
_____

TODAY I PRAY:

TODAY I REGRET:

TODAY I AM IN AWE OF:

TODAY I AM GRATEFUL FOR:

MY *Prayers* FOR: _____
DATE

TODAY I AM ESPECIALLY GRATEFUL FOR:

_____
_____
_____
_____
_____

TODAY I AM PRAYING FOR:

_____
_____
_____
_____
_____
_____
_____
_____
_____
_____
_____
_____

DATE _____

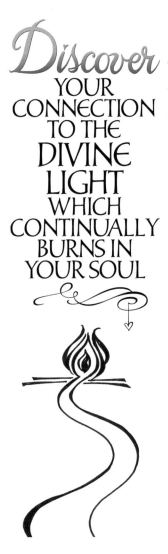

Discover
YOUR
CONNECTION
TO THE
DIVINE
LIGHT
WHICH
CONTINUALLY
BURNS IN
YOUR SOUL

Thank You
FOR BLESSING ME
WITH THE GIFT OF LIFE.

MY  FOR: _____

DATE

TODAY I AM ESPECIALLY GRATEFUL FOR:

_____
_____
_____
_____
_____

TODAY I AM PRAYING FOR:

_____
_____
_____
_____
_____
_____
_____
_____
_____
_____
_____
_____

DATE

TODAY I PRAY:

please

TODAY I AM IN AWE OF:

wow

TODAY I REGRET:

sorry

USE WHICHEVER TYPE OF
PRAYER FEELS RIGHT TO YOU

TODAY I AM GRATEFUL FOR:

thanks

MY *Prayers* FOR: _____
DATE

TODAY I AM ESPECIALLY GRATEFUL FOR:

_____
_____
_____
_____
_____

TODAY I AM PRAYING FOR:

_____
_____
_____
_____
_____
_____
_____
_____
_____
_____
_____
_____
_____

MY *Prayers* FOR: ＿＿＿＿＿＿

TODAY I AM ESPECIALLY GRATEFUL FOR:

_____
_____
_____
_____
_____

TODAY I AM PRAYING FOR:

_____
_____
_____
_____
_____
_____
_____
_____
_____
_____
_____
_____

DATE

TODAY I PRAY:

TODAY I REGRET:

TODAY I AM IN AWE OF:

TODAY I AM GRATEFUL FOR:

MY *Prayers* FOR: _____
DATE

TODAY I AM ESPECIALLY GRATEFUL FOR:

_____
_____
_____
_____
_____

TODAY I AM PRAYING FOR:

_____
_____
_____
_____
_____
_____
_____
_____
_____
_____
_____

LET
YOUR
DIVINE
INNER
FLAME
GLOW SO
BRIGHTLY
IT LIGHTS
A PATH
THAT
OTHERS
MAY
FOLLOW

Thank You

FOR BLESSING ME
WITH THE GIFT OF LIFE.

Reminder:

CHECK YOUR PRAYER LIST

MY  FOR: _____

DATE

TODAY I AM ESPECIALLY GRATEFUL FOR:

_____

_____

_____

_____

_____

TODAY I AM PRAYING FOR:

_____

_____

_____

_____

_____

_____

_____

_____

_____

_____

DATE

TODAY I PRAY:

TODAY I AM IN AWE OF:

TODAY I REGRET:

USE WHICHEVER TYPE OF
PRAYER FEELS RIGHT TO YOU

TODAY I AM GRATEFUL FOR:

MY  FOR: _____

DATE

TODAY I AM ESPECIALLY GRATEFUL FOR:

_____
_____
_____
_____
_____

TODAY I AM PRAYING FOR:

_____
_____
_____
_____
_____
_____
_____
_____
_____
_____
_____
_____
_____

MY  FOR: _____

DATE

TODAY I AM ESPECIALLY GRATEFUL FOR:

_____

_____

_____

_____

_____

TODAY I AM PRAYING FOR:

_____

_____

_____

_____

_____

_____

_____

_____

_____

_____

_____

_____

DATE

TODAY I PRAY:

TODAY I REGRET:

TODAY I AM IN AWE OF:

TODAY I AM GRATEFUL FOR:

MY *Prayers* FOR: _____

TODAY I AM ESPECIALLY GRATEFUL FOR:

TODAY I AM PRAYING FOR:

DATE _____

Create IN ME
A CLEAN HEART
G♥D

PSALM
51:10

_____
_____
_____
_____
_____
_____
_____
_____
_____
_____
_____
_____
_____

Reminder:
CHECK YOUR
PRAYER CALENDAR

MY *Prayers* FOR: _____

TODAY I AM ESPECIALLY GRATEFUL FOR:

_____
_____
_____
_____
_____

TODAY I AM PRAYING FOR:

_____
_____
_____
_____
_____
_____
_____
_____
_____
_____
_____

DATES TO
Remember

Use this perpetual calender to keep track of the dates that are important to the people in your life, and spend sometime coloring it mindfully if you like. Perhaps your sister will be looking forward to celebrating her wedding anniversary, or your friend will be having a hard time on the anniversary of her mother's death (or Mother's Day or her mother's birthday). Reach out as the date approaches and let those you love know you're thinking about them.

You might include: birthdays, wedding anniversaries, dates that loved ones passed on, anniversaries of sobriety, holidays that are meaningful or difficult to someone, job anniversaries, and other dates important to the people in your life.

JANUARY

1 _____
2 _____
3 _____
4 _____
5 _____
6 _____
7 _____
8 _____
9 _____
10 _____
11 _____
12 _____
13 _____
14 _____
15 _____
16 _____
17 _____
18 _____
19 _____
20 _____
21 _____
22 _____
23 _____
24 _____
25 _____
26 _____
27 _____
28 _____
29 _____
30 _____
31 _____

FEBRUARY

1
2
3
4
5
6
7
8
9
10
11
12
13
14
15
16
17
18
19
20
21
22
23
24
25
26
27
28

MARCH

1 _____
2 _____
3 _____
4 _____
5 _____
6 _____
7 _____
8 _____
9 _____
10 _____
11 _____
12 _____
13 _____
14 _____
15 _____
16 _____
17 _____
18 _____
19 _____
20 _____
21 _____
22 _____
23 _____
24 _____
25 _____
26 _____
27 _____
28 _____
29 _____
30 _____
31 _____

1
2
3
4
5
6
7
8
9
10
11
12
13
14
15
16
17
18
19
20
21
22
23
24
25
26
27
28
29
30

MAY

1
2
3
4
5
6
7
8
9
10
11
12
13
14
15
16
17
18
19
20
21
22
23
24
25
26
27
28
29
30
31

JUNE

1
2
3
4
5
6
7
8
9
10
11
12
13
14
15
16
17
18
19
20
21
22
23
24
25
26
27
28
29
30

JULY

1 _____
2 _____
3 _____
4 _____
5 _____
6 _____
7 _____
8 _____
9 _____
10 _____
11 _____
12 _____
13 _____
14 _____
15 _____
16 _____
17 _____
18 _____
19 _____
20 _____
21 _____
22 _____
23 _____
24 _____
25 _____
26 _____
27 _____
28 _____
29 _____
30 _____
31 _____

AUGUST

1 _____
2 _____
3 _____
4 _____
5 _____
6 _____
7 _____
8 _____
9 _____
10 _____
11 _____
12 _____
13 _____
14 _____
15 _____
16 _____
17 _____
18 _____
19 _____
20 _____
21 _____
22 _____
23 _____
24 _____
25 _____
26 _____
27 _____
28 _____
29 _____
30 _____
31 _____

SEPTEMBER

1 _____
2 _____
3 _____
4 _____
5 _____
6 _____
7 _____
8 _____
9 _____
10 _____
11 _____
12 _____
13 _____
14 _____
15 _____
16 _____
17 _____
18 _____
19 _____
20 _____
21 _____
22 _____
23 _____
24 _____
25 _____
26 _____
27 _____
28 _____
29 _____
30 _____

OCTOBER

1
2
3
4
5
6
7
8
9
10
11
12
13
14
15
16
17
18
19
20
21
22
23
24
25
26
27
28
29
30
31

NOVEMBER

1
2
3
4
5
6
7
8
9
10
11
12
13
14
15
16
17
18
19
20
21
22
23
24
25
26
27
28
29
30

DECEMBER

1
2
3
4
5
6
7
8
9
10
11
12
13
14
15
16
17
18
19
20
21
22
23
24
25
26
27
28
29
30
31

P
E
A
C
E

ABOUT THE ARTIST

Joanne Fink, award-winning calligrapher, author, designer, and inspirational speaker, spent most of her career developing products for the gift, stationery, craft and faith-based industries. Her YouTube videos have had more than 1,000,000 views, and her weekly blog encourages people to use their creative talents to make a difference in the world. Joanne's books include *Complete Guide to Bible Journaling: Creative Techniques to Express Your Faith*, *Zenspirations Dangle Designs*, *Expressions of Faith*, *Flowers of Faith*, and her illustrated memoir, *When You Lose Someone You Love*. To see more of Joanne's work, visit *www.zenspirations.com*.

Heartfelt thanks to my friends of different faiths who took the time to review *My Prayer Journal*: Julie Ager, Terri Burket Brown, Gail Beck, Deena Disraelly, Mary Anne Fellows, Cherish Flieder, Laurie Snow Hein, Rabbi Moe Kaprow, Wendy Leech, Penny Lisk, The Reverend Dr. June Maffin, Tracey Lyon Nicholson, Ketra Oberlander, Toni Popkin, Kimme Prindle, Vicki Schreiner, Amy Welday, and Regina Yoder.

ISBN 978-1-64178-003-2

© 2018 by Joanne Fink and Quiet Fox Designs, *www.QuietFoxDesigns.com*, an imprint of Fox Chapel Publishing, 800-457-9112, 903 Square Street, Mount Joy, PA 17552.

My Prayer Journal contains illustrations previously published in *Zenspirations Expressions of Faith*, *L'chaim Celebrate Life*, and *Zenspirations Inspirations*. Background cover image from shutterstock.com

We are always looking for talented authors. To submit an idea, please send a brief inquiry to acquisitions@foxchapelpublishing.com.

Printed in China
Second printing